WASHED AWAY BY FLOODS

CHARLES HOFER

Published in 2018 by The Rosen Publishing Group, Inc.
29 East 21st Street, New York, NY 10010

First Edition

Editor: Melissa Raé Shofner
Book Design: Reann Nye

Photo Credits: Cover, pp. 1, 19 GREGORY BOISSY/AFP/Getty Images; pp. 4–30 (background) John Taylor/EyeEm/Getty Images; p. 4 SWEN PFORTNER/DPA/Getty Images; p. 5 MOHD RASFAN/AFP/Getty Images; p. 7 J. D. Dallet Therin-Weise/age fotostock/Getty Images; p. 9 By elenabsl/Shutterstock.com; pp. 10, 11 Matt Cardy/Getty Images News/Getty Images; p. 13 Win McNamee/Getty Images News/Getty Images; p. 14 Chris Graythen/Getty Images News/Getty Images; p. 15 Handout/Getty Images News/Getty Images; p. 16 Olga Golyazimova/Shutterstock.com; p. 17 The Asahi Shimbun/Getty Images; p. 18 Tony Feder/Getty Images News/Getty Images; p. 19 DianaLundin/E+/Getty Images; p. 21 ALEXANDER NEMENOV/AFP/Getty Images; p. 23 Frans Lemmens/Corbis Unreleased/Getty Images; p. 25 DEA / F. BARBAGALLO/De Agostini Picture Library/Getty Images; p. 26 NICHOLAS KAMM/AFP/Getty Images; p. 27 Hero Images/Getty Images; p. 28 Justin Sullivan/Getty Images News/Getty Images; p. 29 Daniel Berehulak/Getty Images News/Getty Images.

Cataloging-in-Publication Data

Names: Hofer, Charles.
Title: Washed away by floods / Charles Hofer.
Description: New York : PowerKids Press, 2018. | Series: Natural disasters: how people survive | Includes index.
Identifiers: LCCN ISBN 9781538326589 (pbk.) | ISBN 9781538325698 (library bound) | ISBN 9781538326596 (6 pack)
Subjects: LCSH: Floods–Juvenile literature.
Classification: LCC GB1399.H65 2018 | DDC 551.48'9–dc23

Manufactured in the United States of America

CPSIA Compliance Information: Batch #BW18PK: For Further Information contact Rosen Publishing, New York, New York at 1-800-237-9932

CONTENTS

FLOOD ALERT!

Floods have been a problem for humankind since the first civilizations were built thousands of years ago. From long ago to today, raging floodwaters have destroyed cities, spread disease, and taken lives. Even with our current **technologies**, we aren't safe from the dangers of floods.

DISASTER ALERT!

The National Weather Service (NWS) issues alerts when severe weather is possible. NWS warnings are broadcast on television and radio stations to let people know about possible dangers from extreme weather events, such as floods.

4

Floods are a type of natural disaster, or a sudden natural event that may cause great damage and many deaths. Sometimes a flood will grow slowly over several days. Other times, a flood will appear in a matter of seconds, offering no warning before releasing its destructive powers on the land.

Earth will always have floods. However, advances in science and technology are making it easier to **predict** floods and protect ourselves from these dangerous natural disasters.

WHAT IS A FLOOD?

A flood occurs when a large amount of water overflows the area where it's normally contained. Floods often occur during or following heavy rainstorms. These storms may introduce too much water to a natural system that stores or transports water, such as a river or lake. A flood begins when this excess water moves over the banks and spills onto the nearby land, which is called the floodplain.

Excess water may continue to build up and turn into a natural disaster that causes many problems. Towns and cities built near floodplains may easily be flooded. This flooding can cause major damage to buildings and roads. Sometimes people die in floods. Floods can also spread disease, pollute water supplies, and lead to food shortages and power outages.

DISASTER ALERT!

The first stage of the NWS alert system for floods is an advisory. This tells people to be aware of possible flooding in their area.

6

Regular flooding created fertile floodplains along the Nile River. The crops rasied on these floodplains fed the people of Egypt for centuries.

Egyptians and the Nile

Floods can be destructive, but they can also be beneficial. Regular flooding helped ancient Egyptian society flourish for many years. The Nile River—the longest river in the world—ran through the heart of this ancient empire. Each year, the banks of the Nile overflowed. These floodwaters left behind layers of new soil on the Nile's vast floodplain. This rich soil was perfect for growing crops.

THE WATER CYCLE

The water cycle is the continuous process of Earth's water supply moving between the land, oceans, and atmosphere. Much of Earth's water is stored in oceans and mountain snow. Water is also frozen in glaciers and found underground in ancient **aquifers**.

Condensation causes water vapor to form clouds. Earth's water falls from the sky as **precipitation**. The ground may absorb this water, which can refill aquifers. The water may also reach oceans, lakes, or other bodies of water. This water eventually evaporates, or changes from a liquid to a gas, and returns to the atmosphere to begin the cycle again.

Sometimes, however, water builds up in certain areas. If, for example, a rainstorm drops several inches of rain in a short amount of time, all that excess water will need a place to go and a flood may occur.

DISASTER ALERT!

The second stage of the NWS alert system for floods is a watch. The NWS gives alerts when conditions are favorable for flooding and severe floods are possible.

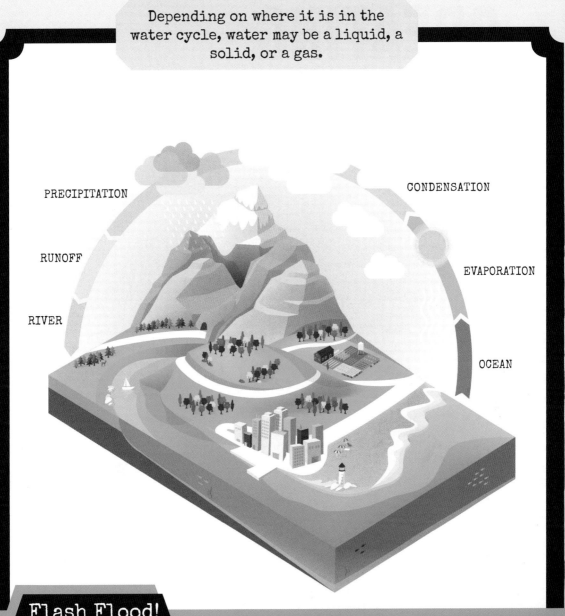

PRECIPITATION

CONDENSATION

RUNOFF

EVAPORATION

RIVER

OCEAN

Flash Flood!

Sometimes a flood can appear almost out of nowhere. These sudden floods are called flash floods. They occur when water builds up quickly in one place, rushing downstream to dry areas. Flash floods are often unexpected and can arrive suddenly with a deadly burst of rushing water. They occur within six hours of a rain event or after a dam or another **barrier**, such as an ice jam, breaks.

9

CREATING
THE FLOOD

The natural areas that capture, store, and transport water—such as rivers and lakes—can help prevent most floods. However, sometimes a series of events can overload these systems. This leads to flooding.

When it rains, the ground may become saturated, or full of water. The ground can't absorb the excess water, which instead pools on the surface. **Nonporous** surfaces,

DISASTER ALERT!

The third and final stage of the NWS alert system for floods is a warning. This means people should take immediate action because a flood is already occurring or is about to occur. This flood could be very dangerous.

10

When water can't sink into the ground because of a paved surface, it may just collect there. This can lead to danger for drivers.

such as paved roads, contribute to floods, too. Water can collect on these hard surfaces and build into a flood.

A lack of vegetation, or plant life, in an area can also contribute to flooding. The root systems of grasses and trees allow the soil to absorb excess water. Without plants, water may flow over the land and collect somewhere else as a flood.

11

WATERSHEDS

The most common type of flood occurs along rivers and streams. These and other water bodies are part of areas of land called watersheds. A watershed is an area in which water collects from various sources. A watershed consists of the land and all the surface water and water located underground. All this water drains into a common location, such as a river at the bottom of the watershed. This river is also part of a watershed and will drain into other, larger rivers or lakes.

Major rain events can create problems in a watershed. If enough rain falls in one area, the waterways in the watershed might become overloaded. These rivers and streams can overflow, sometimes causing horrible flooding.

DISASTER ALERT!

If conditions are right for a flood, it's important to stay safe and seek higher ground. Stay away from places such as basements, valleys, and other low-lying areas where flooding often occurs.

The Mighty Mississippi

Several large rivers, including the Missouri and Ohio Rivers,
empty into the Mississippi River. Because of this, the Mississippi
River is at a high risk for major flooding. In 1927, months of
heavy rain caused the Mississippi River to overflow in the most
destructive river flood in U.S. history. This great flood killed more
than 250 people and forced 600,000 more to leave their homes.

13

COASTAL FLOODS

Coastlines are where the land meets the ocean. They're often large, flat areas at sea level. These are perfect places for floods to occur. Coastal flooding is a serious problem in places such as Florida and the Carolinas. Some weather events, such as hurricanes, can cause a storm surge. A storm surge is when seawater is pushed onto the coastal floodplain by fierce winds. This can cause widespread flooding.

DISASTER ALERT!

Flash floods are the leading cause of weather-related deaths in the United States. In 2016, there were 19 major floods in the United States. This was the highest number of floods in a single year since people started keeping records in 1980.

Hurricane Katrina claimed more than 1,200 lives and caused around $75 billion in damage. This makes it one of the worst natural disasters in United States history.

One of the worst floods in U.S. history struck the city of New Orleans, Louisiana, in August 2005. Hurricane Katrina pounded the city for days, dropping an extraordinary amount of rain. The storm surge from the hurricane, coupled with the rain, flooded the city. The seawalls and other protective barriers meant to hold back floodwaters were no match for Katrina's fury.

SNOWMELT

Another common type of flood results from melting snow. Each winter, snow builds up, forming areas called snowpacks. These fields of snow and ice act as a natural water supply once the snow melts during warmer months.

A sudden burst of warm weather in the spring can cause snowpacks to melt too quickly. This melted snow—called snowmelt—then collects in rivers and streams.

DISASTER ALERT!

Snowmelt provides up to 75 percent of the water supply in the western portion of the United States.

Each year, about 25 to 50 people in the United States die because of mudslides.

Heavy spring rains can add to snowmelt and cause devastating floods. These floods may cause mudslides, which happen when excess water upsets areas of earth on sloping hills and mountains. Mudslides caused by flooding send mud, rocks, and trees sliding downhill, burying everything in their path. Mudslides can damage electrical, water, and gas lines and cover roads and railways.

AFTERMATH

Flood dangers go beyond the damage caused by moving or rising waters. The aftermath of a flood can also cause many problems.

Floods can ruin crops and other food resources. Dirty floodwaters can contaminate, or pollute, fresh water supplies. Without sufficient food and water, flood survivors face new dangers. Washed-out roadways may slow emergency relief, which makes everything worse for flood victims.

DISASTER ALERT!

Walking or driving through floodwaters can be very dangerous. Just a few inches of moving water may knock over a person. A car can be swept away in just 2 feet (0.6 m) of water.

Floodwaters can also take a long time to **recede**. Sometimes these waters carry disease and bacteria. Stagnant, or standing, water can be a breeding ground for mosquitoes, which are known to transmit deadly diseases such as malaria.

Mold is another problem people face after floods. Deadly toxic mold flourishes in dark, damp places and may be present after floodwaters have receded.

DESIGNING FLOOD PROTECTION

People have tried to control the power of water for a long time. Structures such as dams, reservoirs, and canals have helped **engineers** with this task.

Dams are large structures that hold back the flow of river water. Behind a dam, the blocked water is often collected in a man-made lake called a reservoir. When too much water collects in the reservoir, it can be released through the dam in a controlled manner. This system can also provide fresh drinking water and electricity for people living nearby.

Canals are used to reroute the flow of water. These long, man-made trenches are usually lined with concrete or another nonporous material. Canals transport excess water from one place to another, which greatly reduces the possibility of flooding.

DISASTER ALERT!

Avoid areas where floodwaters have recently receded. Floodwaters may make roads, sidewalks, beaches, and riverbanks unstable and unsafe.

The Sayano-Shushenskaya dam, shown here, is located in Russia. The dam is part of the country's largest hydroelectric power plant. Hydroelectricity is electricity made using the power of water.

Flood Control

Today, many major cities have systems in place to help manage floodwaters. Engineers and city planners work together to design a series of underground drains and tunnels that remove excess water from streets, parking lots, and other areas that don't drain well. Storm drains and tunnels move surface water away from cities and towns toward areas such as lakes, rivers, or oceans.

ENGINEERING MARVELS

In some areas where floods are very common, engineers have developed more extreme methods for controlling them. Many cities and towns along the Mississippi River and other major waterways have constructed large barriers to withstand rising river waters during times of flooding. Floodwalls, also called levees, are large walls or raised areas that protect communities from flooding while directing excess water toward safer areas.

Floods are a problem around the world. In the Netherlands, for example, more than half the country's residents live in areas below sea level. For that reason, the country has constructed a series of dams, canals, and other means to protect the land from storm surges. They've even engineered enormous moveable gates that can be closed to block out the surging seawaters.

DISASTER ALERT!

When it comes to floods, it's important to have a plan. You should know your evacuation route as well as the location of your nearest emergency shelter in case floods force you from your home.

The Oosterschelde flood
barrier, shown here, is
located in the Netherlands.

United States Army Corps of Engineers

The United States Army Corps of Engineers (USACE) employs
more than 37,000 people and is one of the world's largest
engineering and management **agencies**. Founded more than
200 years ago, the USACE has played an important part in
developing **infrastructure** around the United States. Over
the years, the USACE has engineered countless dam, canal,
bridge, and tunnel projects that help control floods and help

NATURAL FLOOD PROTECTION

All floods have one thing in common—a lot of water isn't where it's supposed to be. Fortunately, nature had remedies for this long before we built dams and canals to control floodwater.

Wetland areas, such as bogs, swamps, and salt marshes, provide natural protection in areas where floods often occur. These wetlands are often found right next to rivers, lakes, and oceans. Wetlands are important because they work like large sponges to soak up excess water and help reduce flooding.

Barrier islands also work as natural flood protection. These are long, sandy islands located just off the coast. There are many barrier islands along the East Coast of the United States. Barrier islands help reduce the effects of major storm systems, such as hurricanes, during which the storm surge could flood the mainland.

Wetland Protection

Over the last century, the United States has lost more than half its wetlands. Many have been drained so their land could be used for farms, homes, or other buildings. Wetlands are important natural protection from floods. They also clean our water supply by capturing and filtering pollutants from water runoff. Today, many nonprofit companies and government agencies are working to protect and restore wetlands nationwide.

STUDYING
WATER

Protecting ourselves from flooding begins with understanding how water works. Hydrology is the study of water, how it moves across the landscape, and how it's distributed, or spread out, across our planet. Hydrologists are scientists who study water to better understand how water systems work.

Hydrologists use science and math to help solve our water problems. Their studies may be used to protect

DISASTER ALERT!

In the United States, the president can declare a weather event an official natural disaster. About 90 percent of these natural disasters include flooding of some sort.

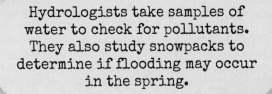

Hydrologists take samples of water to check for pollutants. They also study snowpacks to determine if flooding may occur in the spring.

cities and towns from floods. By working together, hydrologists, engineers, and city planners can design better flood-control systems.

Hydrologists also study the quality and availability of water. Their work helps provide us with clean drinking water and water for agriculture. Hydrologists are looking for ways to meet the ever-growing demand for fresh drinking water around the world.

FLOODS AND CLIMATE CHANGE

Climate change is causing temperatures to increase around the world. Sea levels are rising, and weather is becoming more unpredictable. As a result, terrible floods may become more common—and more destructive.

Places such as Florida and Virginia are already seeing the effects of rising sea levels. Local floods are becoming more frequent. Draining areas and building cities and towns over the land also contributes to this flooding. Long

DISASTER ALERT!
Wildfires are the only natural disaster more widespread in the United States than floods.

periods of **drought** in California have also affected natural flood control systems such as forests and rivers. As a result, sudden rain can have more destructive effects on the landscape.

The effects of floods caused by climate change may be even worse in heavily populated rural places such as Southeast Asia. Flood events can wipe out entire villages in these areas, leaving thousands of people homeless.

FLOOD SAFETY TIPS

Floods are dangerous natural disasters. Follow these tips to stay safe:

- Prepare an emergency kit with food, clean drinking water, and emergency supplies such as a flashlight, first-aid kit, and a battery-powered radio. Keep extra batteries in your kit, too.

- Know your evacuation route and the location of the nearest emergency shelter.

- Use the Internet, television, or radio to receive the latest reports on conditions.

- If there's a flood watch or warning, stay out of low-lying areas.

- Don't walk or drive through flooded areas.

- Throw out any food or drinking water that comes in contact with floodwaters to avoid getting sick.

- Remember to let friends and family know you're safe after a flood.

- Don't return to your home after a flood until officials tell you it's safe to do so.

GLOSSARY

agency: A government department that is responsible for a certain activity or area.

aquifer: A layer of rock or sand that absorbs and holds water.

barrier: Something that blocks something else from passing.

climate change: Change in Earth's weather caused by human activity.

condensation: The process by which water vapor cools and becomes liquid water.

drought: A period of time during which there is very little or no rain.

engineer: Someone who uses math and science to plan and build machines; using math and science to plan and build machines.

infrastructure: The system of public works for a country, state, or region.

nonporous: Not allowing a liquid or gas to pass through.

precipitation: Water that falls to the ground as hail, mist, rain, sleet, or snow.

predict: To guess what will happen in the future based on facts or knowledge.

recede: To move back or away.

technology: A method that uses science to solve problems and the tools used to solve those problems.

INDEX

WEBSITES

Due to the changing nature of Internet links, PowerKids Press has developed an online list of websites related to the subject of this book. This site is updated regularly. Please use this link to access the list: www.powerkidslinks.com/natd/flood